DETECTIVE ACADEMY™

Tracking and Surveillance

by Paul Mauro
with **H. Keith Melton**
consultant

Scholastic Inc.
New York • Toronto • London • Auckland • Sydney
Mexico City • New Delhi • Hong Kong • Buenos Aires

ISBN: 0-439-57180-4

Design: Mark Neston

Illustrations: Daniel Aycock, Yancey Labat, Paul Tutrone, Antoine Clarke

Photos: Nancy Heiberg, Mark Neston

Special thanks to the Nassau County Police Department's Sergeant Donald Stewart, Police Officer Don Carney, Police Officer Frank Leckler, Police Officer Rich Muller—all from the Bureau of Special Operations; Sergeant John Hill and his partner K-9 Chuck from the K-9 unit; and to Chris Roberto, Police Officer Vincent Garcia, and Police Officer Michael Bitsko. Thanks also to Eastern Mountain Sports (EMS) for the compasses photoed on page 25.

12 11 10 9 8 7 6 5 4 3 2 1   4 5 6 7 8 9/0

Printed in the U.S.A.

First Scholastic printing, March 2004

The publisher has made every effort to ensure that the activities in this book are safe when done as instructed. Children are encouraged to do their detective activities with willing friends and family members and to respect others' right to privacy. Adults should provide guidance and supervision whenever the activity requires.

Pictured above is a recording machine used by detectives listening in on conversations while on surveillance.

Case Log

DA When you see this symbol throughout the book, you'll know to use your **detective equipment** in the activity.

 When you see this symbol throughout the book, you'll know there's a related activity to be found on the Detective Academy **website**.

Get on the Trail!

Hey, rookie! Watch where you step! Did you know that, to a trained detective, **tracks** (also known as **footprints**) left on the ground can be almost enough to positively identify you? Tracks can also place you in a particular place at a particular time. Tracks tell your story! In fact, **tracking**—that is, investigating tracks—can be like reading a book, with a criminal's feet telling the tale. And because tracks tell a detective so much (especially if they're matched to a particular suspect), they can make excellent evidence in a criminal case.

In order to be a full-fledged detective, rookie, you'll learn how to find, preserve, and analyze track evidence. You'll also learn how to conduct **surveillance** on someone you suspect of committing a crime. And that's what this book is all about. So, prepare to undergo your complete track and surveillance training!

THE TALE OF THE TRACKS

As you probably already know, you don't always leave tracks when you walk around. Because we spend most of our time walking on surfaces like concrete or grass, we don't usually leave very clear tracks. But to a detective, that's usually not a problem! That's because, in many cases, the **perpetrator** of a crime *does* walk through something that leaves tracks at some point—whether he realizes it or not!

For instance, let's say a perp commits a burglary of a house. Chances are he didn't just walk up to the front door and ring the doorbell! A perp committing this type of crime will usually break into the house through a window. And that means walking through flowerbeds or other soil areas that usually surround a house. And that means...footprint tracks!

But there's another common way that criminals leave tracks. Instead of leaving a footprint in soft sand, soil, or snow, they sometimes pick up dirt or liquid on their shoes and leave a track on a hard surface. So even if that burglar didn't leave a footprint in the soil *outside* the house, chances are his shoes got dirty enough that he left a footprint *inside* the house!

Whether left in soft soil or on a hard surface, footprint evidence is only as good as the detective investigating it! The detective has got to know where to find the tracks, how to process them, and how to use them to narrow down the search for **suspects**. All techniques you'll learn in this book.

THE ART OF SURVEILLANCE

With tracking, rookie, the detective is attempting to find a suspect based on the footprints he left behind. With surveillance, however, the detective doesn't have to find the suspect. Why? Because the suspect is right there in front of her!

Tracks found on concrete (above) and in snow (below).

When a detective conducts a surveillance, she's watching a suspect or group of suspects without the suspect (or suspects) knowing it. Like tracking, it's all about following the suspect and keeping your eyes open. But with surveillance, the detective either isn't sure she has the right suspect or she wants to learn more about him and anyone he associates with. So she secretly watches him—either using high-tech equipment or clever detective techniques that allow her to get close to him but still stay hidden. Techniques you're about to learn!

Detectives on a roof-top surveillance.

So whether you're tracking a suspect by following his footprints, or conducting a surveillance by secretly watching him, it's all about using your training and powers of observation to learn as much as you can. Then, when you've learned enough, it's time to make the **collar**!

Are you ready to start developing your tracking and surveillance skills?

DA Detective Equipment

This month, rookie, you're receiving special gear to help you find suspects, and to keep track of—and an eye on—them!

- **A compass**—which allows you to determine which direction a suspect under surveillance is headed.

- **Evidence markers**—which allow you to mark a path and return to the track evidence you discover.

- **A Mylar sheet and wool cloth**—to help you preserve even faint tracks found in dust.

- **Casting powder**—to make permanent **casts** of tracks you discover.

Detective Academy Website

For more on tracking and surveillance, rookie—including additional training exercises and a whole new case to solve—visit the Detective Academy website at **www.scholastic.com/detective**. Remember: You'll need your password to access this month's website! Your special tracking and surveillance password is: **TAGTEAM**.

PASSWORD: TAGTEAM

TRACKING A SUSPECT

Detectives on a case can **track** a **suspect** from a crime scene—like this one, of a robbery at an electronics store—by carefully examining any **footprints** they find. This is the first step in tracking a suspect—getting an idea of where he went!

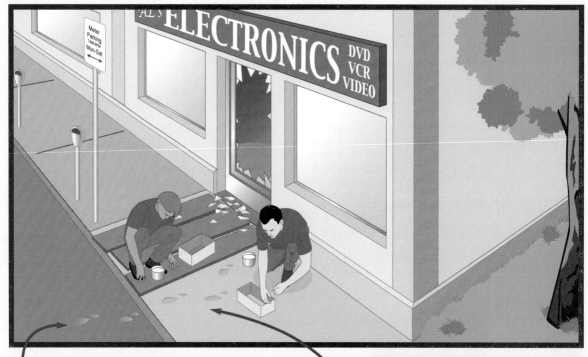

DIRECTION OF FLIGHT

By following a suspect's tracks, detectives can also learn about his direction and method of flight. Footprints that end suddenly might indicate a suspect entered a car or other vehicle. (And if they entered a car's passenger side, that means someone *else* was driving—the **perp** had a partner!)

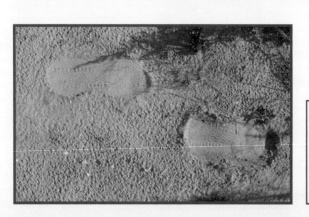

TRACKS IN THE GROUND

Tracks made by a suspect in soft ground can tell detectives things like shoe size, type of shoe worn—sometimes even the perp's height and weight. These footprints will be preserved as valuable evidence to be studied at length later.

But these days, tracking a suspect means more than just looking at his footprints. Today, detectives can use computer technology to follow a suspect's movements from afar.

So if an electronics store has been robbed and a perpetrator has stolen some cell phones...detectives may be able to track that perp if he (or one of his buddies) uses one of those phones.

TRACKING CELL PHONES

With the permission of a judge, detectives can access a cell phone company's broadcast system—and pinpoint the location of a cell phone caller.

PHONE TAPS

Detectives can also, with a judge's permission, tap a suspect's cell phone or regular phone—and digitally record all phone calls made and received by that phone.

SUSPECT'S MOVEMENTS

Detectives track a suspect's movements on a map—familiarizing themselves with his goings on.

REVERSE PHONE BOOKS

Special "reverse phone books" allow detectives to look up a phone number first, then find out who it belongs to. Using these books—or special computer programs that work in a similar way—detectives can track down who the owner of any phone number is that a suspect calls (and so, keep track of who the suspect's associating with).

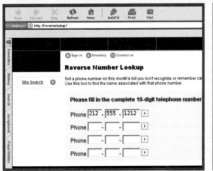

PERSONAL DOCUMENTS

Also with the permission of a judge, detectives can get copies of a suspect's personal records—like bank statements, credit card records, and phone bills. By examining where a suspect has been using his credit or ATM cards, detectives can track where that suspect has been—and so, where he might be going.

SURVEILLING A SUSPECT

Surveillance is different from **tracking**, rookie—because you already have the **suspect** in sight! But just because you see him, doesn't mean you want *him* to see *you*.

So if detectives develop a suspect by tracking a stolen cell phone, but they don't have enough evidence to arrest him yet—or if they want to see if he's part of a criminal gang—they can use special techniques for staying hidden while they keep him under surveillance.

HAND SIGNALS

Detectives **tailing** a suspect will sometimes use hand signals to indicate a suspect's movements. If the detectives are **tag teaming**, running a hand through their hair may indicate it's time for one detective to back off as the other takes over the surveillance. Here, the photo on the left shows the detective indicating that the suspect has made a right turn. In the photo on the right, she indicates that the suspect has stopped.

SWITCH OFF

The second half of a tag team will respond to the signal to **hand-off** by walking past his partner and taking over the surveillance. This keeps the suspect from noticing the same person following him.

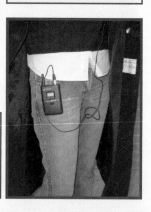

HIDDEN MICROPHONE

Detectives will sometimes use a microphone hidden in their clothing in order to keep in contact with other detectives nearby. The microphone is connected to a portable police radio, also hidden somewhere in the detective's pockets. (You can see them photoed here, but a **perp** wouldn't be able to!)

Sometimes detectives will conduct a surveillance on a particular location—if they think the location is connected to criminal activity. So if a suspect is known to visit a particular house often—or if the detectives have determined he's been calling there very often, they may place that location under surveillance for weeks at a time.

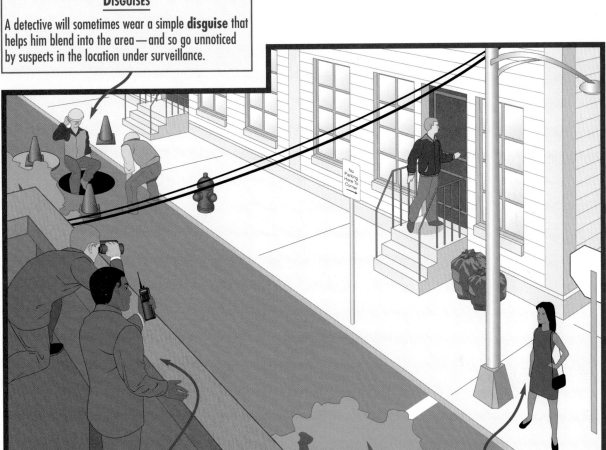

DISGUISES

A detective will sometimes wear a simple **disguise** that helps him blend into the area—and so go unnoticed by suspects in the location under surveillance.

OBSERVATION POST

Detectives will sometimes set up an **observation post**, where they can remain out of sight while they watch a particular location. Detectives in the "o.p." will keep in contact with the detectives on the ground by police radio—so everyone knows what the suspect is doing at all times.

MOVING ON!

The detective who's been tailing the suspect will now exit the area, leaving the surveillance to the detective in the hand-off. After following the suspect, she can't be seen hanging around the surveillance location. The suspect might get suspicious!

DETECTIVE JARGON

Here are this month's tracking and surveillance jargon words. Look for them in **bold** throughout the book.

Cast: The object formed by a mold. When plaster is poured into the mold, it creates a cast.

Casting Powder: Water is added to this dry substance to form plaster to make a cast of footprint impressions.

To Collar: To make an arrest.

Disguise: To change your appearance so that you aren't recognized.

Elimination Prints: A shoe casting taken by detectives from the victim of a crime to differentiate the victim's footprints from those of a potential suspect.

Evidence Markers: Detectives use these to show where they've found small bits of evidence, making it easy to find the evidence again.

First Responders: Uniformed police officers who are the first to respond when someone calls the police.

The Follow: To walk or drive behind a suspect, and to observe his actions.

Footprints: Tracks left on the ground by someone's feet. These can be either impressions in dirt or sand, or on a hard surface, or can also be made from a liquid someone has walked through.

To Get Burned: When a detective is noticed by a suspect she's tailing or conducting surveillance on.

Hand-off: During a follow, when one detective lets another take over the surveillance of the suspect.

A Hook: An obvious part of someone's appearance—like a bright hat or sweatshirt—that is then removed or replaced, in order to disguise that person.

Impressions: A mark made by pressure—usually, of someone's feet on soft ground.

Kidnapping: A crime in which a perp takes someone captive by force.

Mold: An impression in the ground (like a footprint) into which you pour plaster to make a cast.

Observation Post: An area from which detectives can conduct surveillance on a suspect or suspicious area.

Perpetrator or **Perp:** A person guilty of committing a crime.

To Scout: A careful detective will take an early look at an area where a surveillance or follow will occur, before it occurs.

Surveillance: The close study or observation—in secret—of a suspect or area.

Suspect: A person who may have committed a crime, who might be the perpetrator.

Tag Team: When more than one detective tails a suspect, switching off every now and then to avoid being spotted.

Tail: To follow a suspect during a surveillance.

To Take Down: To make a number of arrests, usually of members of a criminal gang or organization.

Tracking: Using footprints or other evidence, like broken twigs or dropped evidence, to follow a suspect.

Tracks: Impressions such as footprints or tire prints left by a suspect.

Treads: The design on the bottom of a shoe or sneaker.

You're Getting Warmer...!

Rookie, **tracking** and **surveillance** are two sides of the same coin—they both involve *observation*. Even though most of us do this all the time (how about the surveillance you conduct on that classmate you have a crush on?), there's a bit more to it than what you're used to! To track and conduct surveillance the way detectives do, you have to step it up a bit!

Try these two short "warm-up" activities to start learning how tracking and surveillance are a bit more than just "keeping an eye on someone"!

TRACKING

Most of us see **tracks** every day, rookie—we just don't usually *notice* them. So to start becoming track-sensitive, take a look around your house, both inside and outside. Can you find any tracks? Check outside areas where the ground is soft, and inside areas where there may be some dust. Can you find any **footprints**? Can you tell who made them? Are they yours? A family member's? How do you know?

Then take a walk around your neighborhood looking for other tracks. Once you find some, see if you can make any guesses as to who made them. Was it an adult or a child? A teenager? Pay attention to who usually walks in the place where you find the tracks. Does that help you guess what type of person might have made them? Do you see any animal tracks? Follow the **impressions** as far as you can. Where do you think the person was going? Were they alone or with someone?

The first step in becoming an effective "track reader," rookie, is to start *noticing* tracks—and to practice observing as many of them as you can!

SURVEILLANCE

Surveillance can be a difficult skill to perfect. There are some very specific techniques that you'll need. But that's what Detective Academy is all about!

To start your surveillance training, begin by picking out a friend or classmate to observe. You don't need to follow them. Just pick someone you see every day—but now, *really* watch them. Do they have any nervous habits? Do they always look tired? Do they fall asleep in class? Are they always tapping one foot, or constantly biting their fingernails? Don't stop the surveillance until you discover something about that person that you never noticed before. Then try it out on another person. Are you surprised how much you're suddenly learning about people you thought you knew?

Not Exactly a Walk in the Park!

When a detective is **tracking** a **suspect**, rookie, he has to follow that suspect —no matter where he goes. And if that means mud, then that means mud! (A detective isn't exactly asked his opinion on this, you know!)

But an even more difficult place for a detective to track a suspect is through a wooded area. If a suspect has fled through an area with lots of trees, tracking the suspect is going to be tougher than in sand or mud. The ground in a wooded area is often firmer than sand, so **footprints** won't show up as clearly. Plus, trees and bushes in woods mean lots of leaves and twigs on the ground—things that can also be confusing when trying to track a **perp**. But these leaves and twigs can actually *help* you track someone, too. Keep reading to see how!

What You Do

Part I. Two's Company, Tree's a Crowd

1. First, rookie, you'll need a wooded area! So ask a senior detective (as in, *a parent*) if there's a safe, wooded place nearby where you can practice your detective skills. (Maybe they want to come along!) Make sure you try this activity during the daytime—you can't track someone if you can't see what you're doing!

2. Once you're in the woods, have your fellow rookie walk along ahead of you while you follow a few steps behind. Make note of any marks he makes as he walks. Does he leave footprints? Does he kick up a lot of leaves as he walks? How does he disturb the ground that he walks past? Does he break any branches or twigs? (*That's* how leaves and twigs can help you track a suspect!)

3. Now that you've warmed up a bit, turn your back on your friend as he walks ahead. Tell him you'll give him a few minutes head start, then he should hide behind a tree.

4. After you've given him enough time (count to 150 or so—that should be enough), turn around and see if you can track him down. Look for the same things on the ground you saw when you were walking right behind him—scattered leaves, broken twigs, partial footprints. If he were a suspect in a crime, would you be able to find him?

5. Once you're done, switch roles. As the "suspect," can you hide from your friend without leaving enough clues for him to track?

Part II. Leaving Your Mark

As a detective, there's a chance that you could be on a case where the person you're tracking *wants* to be found! In a case of a **kidnapping**, for instance, the victim may intentionally leave clues for you to follow— in hopes of being found and rescued.

1. This activity works best in the woods, rookie, but you don't *have* to do it there. Your backyard, the beach, or your neighborhood block all work. But be sure to decide with your fellow rookie on the boundaries of where you'll be searching. (Don't make it too large. After all, you don't have a whole police department to help you, like a professional detective might!)

2. Your friend will be leaving clues to help you track him, and you'll be the detective following him. So first, agree on some markers that your friend can leave for you to follow. They could be rocks that have obviously been moved, tree branches laid a certain way, a small pile of leaves or pebbles...use your imagination. (Think: What would *you* use if you were trying to help a detective find you?)

3. Next, give your friend a good head start. He should have about three to five minutes or so to get ahead of you before he finds a spot to hide and waits for you to find him. Make sure he leaves the markers along the way to help guide you.

4. Now, see if you can track him down. Carry your **evidence markers** with you. As you find the markers your friend left for you, leave an evidence marker to point out each one.

5. If you have another rookie practicing with you, tell her to follow after *you* after five minutes or so. Can *she* spot any clues you missed? Can she follow *both* of you by the evidence markers you've left? If you've been tracking well, all three of you should end up in the same spot!

What's the Real Deal?

It can be tough to track someone through a wooded area! Because of all the branches, twigs, leaves, and rocks, spotting clear footprints on the ground can be difficult. Even if someone is leaving clues for you, it can still be tricky! But if you watch carefully, those branches, leaves, and twigs can sometimes show you where a suspect has been walking.

A detective tracking in an area like this would often rely on a number of possible helpers to make the job easier. A *canine* unit (sometimes abbreviated as "K-9") is a special police team that uses highly trained dogs to follow the scent of who ever is being tracked. (See below for more on these remarkable animals!) In very serious cases in remote areas of the country, special Native American trackers might even be called in to help the search. (Check page 44 to meet one of these specialists.) But if a detective is on her own trying to track someone in the woods, she's going to rely on the same techniques you just practiced.

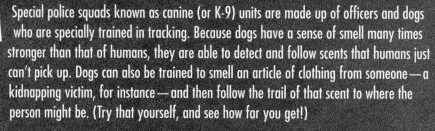

JUST THE FACTS

K-9 Sometimes, rookie, detectives need a little non-human help when tracking a suspect. That's when they "go to the dogs"!

Special police squads known as canine (or K-9) units are made up of officers and dogs who are specially trained in tracking. Because dogs have a sense of smell many times stronger than that of humans, they are able to detect and follow scents that humans just can't pick up. Dogs can also be trained to smell an article of clothing from someone—a kidnapping victim, for instance—and then follow the trail of that scent to where the person might be. (Try that yourself, and see how far you get!)

Different types of dogs are generally used for different types of police duties. For instance, when tracking a person who is lost or missing, police will often use a breed of dog known as a bloodhound. The dog's handler will first allow the dog to sniff an article of clothing from the person—an old shirt, for example, or a hat. The bloodhound will then automatically search for the person who matches that scent. Other breeds of dogs—like the larger German shepherd, for instance—are trained to track the freshest human scent they find. This makes them excellent for finding people suddenly trapped in burned or collapsed buildings. (Their size also makes them effective for apprehending perps. German shepherds can be trained to take down a fleeing or resisting perp—without seriously injuring him.)

Other breeds of dog can be trained to do police work—including the powerful rottweilers and the intelligent labradors. These breeds—again, along with the trusty German shepherds—are often used to detect hidden explosives or narcotics. Canine units are so effective at tracking because of a unique combination: They not only have an amazing sense of smell, they're also intelligent animals—and can be trained. Which truly makes them a detective's best friend!

A Moldy but Goody

Rookie, when a detective **tracks** a **suspect** the detective will nearly always want to preserve the suspect's **footprints** as evidence. That way, the prints can be looked at carefully to see if they provide any more information about the suspect. And if a suspect is eventually caught, the detective can then match the footprints to the suspect's shoes, confirming they have the right **perp**. When track evidence is present in an investigation, it *must* be recorded!

Crime scene techs will usually take photos of the footprints, but in most cases, photos just aren't enough. A better way to preserve tracks is to make a **cast** of them. Using a specially designed, plaster-like mixture, detectives make casts of a suspect's footprints. They then have a three-dimensional representation of every detail of those tracks.

Knowing how to record track evidence is a key detective skill. Give it a try with this activity!

What You Do

Part I. I've Been "Framed"!

1. You can either use a footprint you or your friend already made in *Case File #1: Not Exactly a Walk in the Park!*, or you can make a new one. Just be sure to step down firmly, to get a nice, deep **impression** of your shoe. (This activity is similar to the one in the Detective Academy *Prints and Impressions* book. But this time, rookie, you'll be focusing more on tracking. It just demonstrates how a detective's many skills rely on each other for a complete investigation!)

2. You'll need four pieces of good, strong cardboard. Cut four pieces that are big enough to "frame" the footprint—that is, to make a tight rectangle around it.

3. Grease one side of each piece of the cardboard with the petroleum jelly. Then frame the footprint with the cardboard, keeping the greased side in. Make sure the ends of each cardboard piece are touching, so that when you pour the **casting powder** in, it won't leak out!

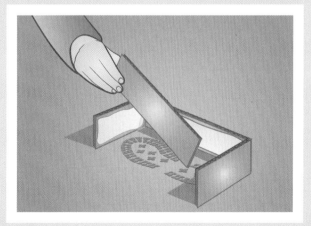

4. Open your jar of casting powder and fill the lid with water. Pour it into the jar with the powder mixture. Do this again. Then close the jar and shake it up until the powder turns into a liquid.

5. Open the jar and pour the liquid you've made into the cardboard square you formed around the footprint. Fill in the footprint completely.

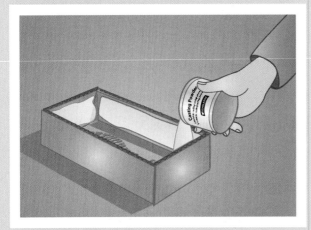

6. Now, write the date in the liquid (after it's set a bit) using a pencil. Use abbreviations: If it's October 23, 2004, write the date this way: 10-23-04. (You now have a permanent record of when you made this footprint cast—carved into the cast itself!) In your detective notebook, also record the time of day you made the cast, and the address of where it was made. (A detective has to keep "track" of all her **tracks**. This way, the evidence can't be challenged later by a suspect claiming to be innocent!)

7. Next, take your compass and determine the direction in which the toe of the footprint is pointing. (Go to page 27, "How to Use Your Compass," for more info on how to understand your gadget.)

Record the letter for the direction right in your mold, using the pencil (so if the toe is facing west, just write "W").

8. Let the mold mixture dry! In about an hour, remove the cardboard sidings and lift the cast gently out of the ground. Brush off any excess dirt that clings to it. It should have hardened into a perfect likeness of the footprint on the bottom, and the date and direction it was facing on the top. This not only gives you a strong piece of evidence, it gives you a *well-recorded*, properly documented piece of evidence as well. You know when you got the print, and which way it was facing. This is the kind of clue any detective loves to have!

Part II. Learning to "Type"

Part of using track evidence to identify a suspect, rookie, is learning what *type* of shoe the suspect was wearing. By examining a footprint, an experienced detective can often tell if the suspect was wearing sneakers, boots, high heels, or some other footwear. And knowing what a suspect wears on his feet can be an important clue as to who he is!

1. First, see how many different shoe types you can gather from around your house. Try to get at least one sample from each of the following: sneakers, boots, high heels, flip-flops, loafers, and any other unusual or interesting types that you can find. See if you can get a good mix of male and female shoes, as well.

2. Now, using the same process you used in *Part I*, make a cast from each of these shoe types. Remember to start by pressing hard into the ground to make a nice, clear footprint to work with. (And don't forget to grease the cardboard!) To make more casting powder, follow the recipe below.

3. As you make the casts, don't forget to label each one with the shoe type, so that you can tell them apart later on. Use your pencil to record this info right in the cast's top. Again, use abbreviations to make it easier: "hh" can be high heels, "s" can stand for sneaker...you get the idea!

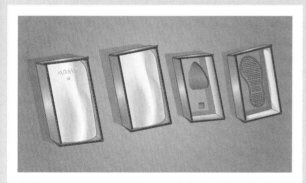

4. Once each cast has dried, remove it and brush it off so you can see it clearly. Then compare the casts to each other. Can you tell them apart? Would you be able to tell what type of shoe made each one?

5. Now that you have a permanent catalog of a bunch of different shoe types, it's time to test your knowledge. Invite a fellow rookie to help. Have your friend show you one cast at a time so you can only see the bottom where the shoe impression is. Can you determine what type of shoe each is? When you're done, switch roles and let your friend give it a try!

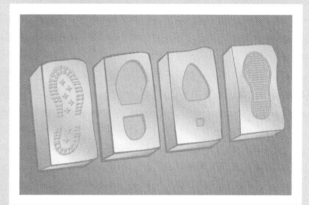

More Casting Powder Mix!

If you want to keep practicing with footprint casts, rookie, you'll need a good supply of casting powder. So use this recipe whenever you need another batch. It makes just enough for one shoe print.

1. You should make the mixture just before you plan to use it, rookie. (Casting powder doesn't "keep" in the refrigerator like leftovers!) You can mix it at home, then fill your casting powder jar to take it with you to wherever you're going to make your footprint cast.

2. You'll need the following ingredients:
   2 cups of baking soda
   1 cup of cornstarch
   $1^1/_3$ cups of warm water

3. Mix the baking soda and the cornstarch in a saucepan. Add the water, and keep stirring while — *with the help of a senior detective* — you warm the mix, over medium heat on the stove for about two minutes.

4. Let the mix cool down a bit, then pour it into your casting powder jar. You're now ready to start casting!

More From Detective Squad

Another reason to make casts of the shoes around your house, rookie, is to practice taking **elimination prints**. Detectives usually take elimination prints from the victim at a crime scene so that they can tell which tracks were made by the victim, and which were made by the suspects. That way, detectives don't waste time investigating the wrong tracks!

Just in case you ever have to investigate some unknown tracks around your house, why not make a catalog of elimination prints of everyone living with you? First, get permission from a senior detective to use some shoes from around the house. Start by pressing a shoe from each pair you find onto some hard soil.

After pressing on the ground, press that shoe onto a blank sheet of clean white typing paper. That will give you a good impression of that shoe's bottom. Label it at the top, "Dad's work shoe" or "Mom's sneaker." (Just be sure to use hard soil, and not mud, rookie. You don't want to ruin anyone's good shoes!) When you're done, put all the sheets in a folder or binder marked "Elimination Prints."

When anyone in your family gets new shoes in the future, ask them to let you take an elimination print to add to your file. Now if there's ever an investigation into unidentified tracks near your house, you've got a complete record of elimination prints ready to go!

What's the Real Deal?

All this mixing and pouring had a purpose, rookie! The idea was for you not only to see how to make a cast of a shoe impression, but to learn something about how to use that cast as evidence. By making good, accurate footprint casts and then learning what shoe types probably made them, you've taken a big "step" in interpreting track evidence!

Detectives who encounter footprints at a crime scene, or from a suspect they've been tracking, make casts just like you did in this activity. There really is no better way to preserve a piece of evidence like this (especially when you consider this clue—a footprint—is going to disappear as soon as it rains or someone walks over it!). By making a permanent record, detectives now have evidence they can match to a suspect in the future. They can also use this clue to make educated guesses about the suspect. After all, what you wear on your feet can tell a lot about you. Shoe type and size can often tell a detective a suspect's gender, and even approximate body size. Which is all excellent information to have (bet you didn't realize that feet could "say" so much!).

Making Tracks

As you learned in *Case File #2: A Moldy but Goody*, making a plaster **cast** of **footprints** is an excellent way of preserving important evidence. But just as different shoes can affect what a footprint looks like, different *locations* can do that, too. If the **tracks** a detective finds are in sand, they're going to look different from tracks found in grass or mud. Different locations also affect the process of making a cast of those footprints—and what the final cast will look like, as well.

Try this out to get a feel for it!

Stuff You'll Need
- Shoes with treads in the soles
- Evidence markers DA
- Casting powder DA
- Cardboard
- Petroleum jelly
- Pencil DA
- A fellow rookie
- 5 or 6 index cards
- Ruler

What You Do

Part I. Have Casts, Will Travel!

1. First, select a shoe that you know will give you a good footprint. It should have clear, well-formed **treads** on the bottom, so that any prints you make with it will show a clear pattern.

2. Now, select a few different locations—like the grass on your lawn, a hard-packed dirt spot, a muddy spot, and some sand. Make a footprint in each place, using the same shoe. Remember to press down firmly so you get a good, clear **impression**.

Hard-packed dirt

Grass

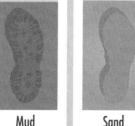

Mud

Sand

3. Mark each footprint with one of your **evidence markers** so that you can return to the prints easily, and so that they won't be disturbed.

4. Once you've got a few good footprints made using the same shoe, use the same method from *Case File #2: A Moldy but Goody* to make a cast of each impression. Remember to grease the cardboard so that the final cast slides out easily!

5. While the casts are still wet, use a pencil to write the location where it was made. (Use abbreviations, rookie—"G" can stand for grassy area, "HD" for hard dirt, and so on.)

6. Once all the casts are dry, remove them by gently lifting them out of the cardboard and brushing aside any excess sand or dirt.

7. Now lay the casts down side-by-side, with the footprint side facing up at you. Can you tell the difference between them? Is it clear which surface makes for a better footprint casting? How do the casts differ? Are there some characteristics of your footprint that

are clear in one of the casts, but not the others?

8. Try mixing up the casts (or have a fellow rookie or family member do it for you).

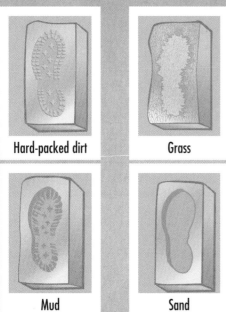

Hard-packed dirt

Grass

Mud

Sand

When you examine them again, can you tell which surface made which print? One of these surfaces is much harder to get casts from than the others, rookie. Do you know which one? Check *Case Closed* to see if you're right.

Part II. A Hop, Skip, and a Jump!

Another way that casts of footprints can differ is due to the way the person who made them was *moving*. Tracks made by a person who is running hard will look different from those made by someone who is just casually strolling along. How will they look different? Try the following activity to find out!

1. First, put on a pair of shoes that are good for making prints. Then, find an area of nice, soft soil that will hold footprints well.

2. Make footprints in this area the following ways: by walking, running, hopping up and down, jumping from one spot to another, and walking backward. Label each footprint type by writing how you made it on an index card, and laying it next to those prints.

3. Now, using a ruler, measure the *depth* of each footprint (that is, how deep each one is). What do you notice about how the depth differs between the prints? Check the prints for clarity, too. Are some prints easier to "read" than others? Which give the clearest impression of the bottom of your shoe, and which are the most smudged? Why do you think that is? (When you're done examining these prints, check *Case Closed* for what you should have observed!)

What's the Real Deal?

Tired from all that jumping and hopping, rookie? You should be! But it was for a good cause. This activity was all about the different factors that can affect what tracks look like. Just as different shoes leave different-looking tracks, so, too, will the same shoe in different surfaces. A suspect running will also leave tracks that look different from that same suspect walking. As you can see, when examining tracks, there are a lot of factors to consider!

For a real detective working a case, rookie, the main concern with a footprint will almost always be *clarity*. The detective will want a footprint that shows—as clearly as possible—what the pattern is on the sole of the shoe that made it. That's why the surface that a print is found in is so important. A detective will always prefer prints made in material that is soft, but still firm—like soil in a backyard garden, for instance. But because footprints can be such valuable evidence, detectives will go to any lengths to reveal them. Check out the next Case File, for an example of how an experienced detective can coax a footprint out of almost nothing!

CASE IN POINT A Really "Big" Clue!

As you've learned, rookie, the last thing a criminal wants to leave at a crime scene is a footprint. It's a clue that can be valuable to a detective. But some footprints can be worse for a **perp** than others!

In a case in Vermont in 2003, a perp burglarized a drug store by breaking into the shop next door, then tunneling into the drug store. The criminal then made off with over $16,000 worth of merchandise. Because he'd bypassed the drug store's security system, it looked like the clever crook might get away with it!

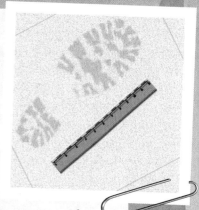

But that was *before* detectives discovered a clue at the scene: a single dusty footprint. The detectives knew that a known criminal was in the area where the crime was committed, so they began concentrating their investigation on him. When they found out a key fact about the suspect, they knew they were on the right *track*!

It seems that the known criminal had enormous feet—size 13! The dusty footprint found at the drug store was also huge—exactly size 13. The detectives had a perfect match! A search of the known criminal's home and car uncovered evidence of the crime, and the man was arrested and charged with burglary.

It was a case of detectives using track evidence effectively—and a perp whose feet are just too big for his current line of work!

Magic Dust

Rookie, there are a number of ways that a detective can record **tracks** of a **suspect** she's pursuing. If the prints are made in something soft, like soil, then a **cast** is best (as you learned in *Case File #3: Making Tracks*). If a **perp's footprints** are made on something hard, however—like a cement sidewalk—photographing them is the best way to go because there aren't any **impressions** to fill with **casting powder**. Think that covers all the possibilities? Not so fast!

Another common place a suspect's tracks can be discovered is in dust. A perp who has entered a home or building through a long-unused window or doorway may leave tracks in the dust that has gathered there. Very often the perp won't even realize he's left these tracks because they're so hard to see. Footprints in dust can be very faint. But that doesn't mean they aren't there. You just have to know how to tease them out!

What You Do

Part I. Into the Dust

1. First, find an area of your house that's a bit dusty. Try the attic, or maybe a corner in your basement or garage. You could even try the back of a closet.

2. Then, without stepping on the dusty area, bend down and shine a flashlight across the floor at a horizontal angle. Do you see any footprints in the dust? Turn out the room lights to help you see better. Do you see any prints now?

3. If you don't see any (or the prints aren't very clear), take a few steps in the dusty area, then examine the area again. *Now* do you see the footprints? Turn on the room lights again. The prints are much tougher to see now, aren't they?

Part II. Out of the Dust

1. Now, it's time for some tracking magic! Place your Mylar, shiny side up, over one of the dusty footprints.

2. Using the wool, gently rub back and forth across the top of the Mylar, while holding it in place over the footprint.

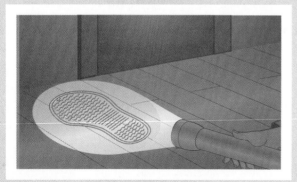

3. Once you've rubbed back and forth over the footprint a few times, lift up the Mylar sheet and gently flip it over. Shine your flashlight on the sheet, holding the light so that the beam strikes the Mylar at an angle. (Do this in dim lighting for best results.) Do you see the dusty footprint there, transferred from the floor to the Mylar sheet? Congratulations! One piece of tracking evidence successfully captured!

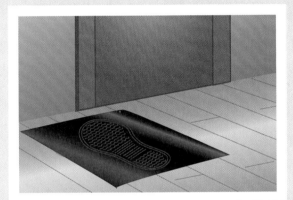

More From Detective Squad

If you used the same shoe to make both the dusty footprint and a cast from one of the previous Case Files, you can learn a lot by comparing the Mylar and the cast. (If you didn't use the same shoe to make both, why not mix up some casting powder and make a cast of the shoe right now?) Once you've got both a cast and a dust impression of the same shoe, you can lay them side by side and compare them. What is the difference between them? Do they share all the same features? Or does one impression show things the other doesn't?

What's the Real Deal?

This activity was all about the equipment, rookie—how to use the Mylar-and-wool technique to permanently capture a perp's footprints that were formed in dust. The key is to rub gently and cover the whole print. Because the dust sticks to the Mylar, a good impression of that footprint can be transferred. Did you see how clear a dusty footprint can be? Surprising, isn't it?

A real detective knows to look in dusty areas for footprints. Remember: Criminals will often enter a house or other building in the way least likely to be seen. And this often means using an old garage door or basement window. And that also means: dust...and dusty footprints! Using the Mylar-and-wool method, detectives can make sure these footprints become permanent clues in the case—rather than ending up in a vacuum cleaner!

Four "Points" You Need to Know!

Stuff You'll Need
- Compass DA
- Evidence markers DA
- Pencil DA
- Notebook DA
- A quarter
- A rookie friend

Rookie, a big part of **tracking** down a **suspect** is getting as much help as you can. Unfortunately, the suspect has one built-in advantage: you're following *him*, so he always gets to make the first move!

In order to do all they can to track down a suspect, police rarely go it alone. If the **perp** has been surprised while committing a crime, the **first responders** will get on their radios and call more officers to come help. If a detective is later tracking a suspect who got away, he, too, will stay in radio contact with other police personnel who are lending a hand. And when talking to each other about the direction the perp fled in, police *always* use what are known as "compass directions"—that is, north, south, east, and west. A typical police radio broadcast might sound like this: "Perp fled east on Caton Avenue, then south on Flatbush Avenue. Perp last seen heading south on Flatbush!" All police officers listening in on the radio would now know *exactly* where that perpetrator is. They know where to respond, instead of just running all over town looking for him!

Police use the four points of a compass to give directions all the time, rookie—whether they're chasing a suspect, tracking him after he's gotten away, or secretly watching him while conducting **surveillance** (another skill you'll soon learn all about!). As a rookie trainee, you need to start giving directions this way, too.

So first check out the "How to Use Your Compass" section on page 27, to get a feel for how to "read" this simple—but effective!—piece of equipment. When you're done, try the activity below. By the time you're finished, you'll be able to track a perp to the four corners of the Earth!

What You Do

Part I. Track and Field

1. First, you and your fellow rookie need to find a nice, open area to practice in—an empty ball field in a park is perfect.

2. Next, use one of your **evidence markers** to designate your "starting point." Put the marker at your feet. Then, while your friend covers her eyes so she can't see what you're doing, take your compass

(orient it north, first, so you know where you're going) and walk a certain number

of steps in one direction (for instance, "six steps south"). Write down the number of steps you took, and in which direction, in your notebook.

3. Then, turn and walk in a new direction. After a certain number of steps, stop and again write down how many steps you took and in which direction.

4. Do this five or six times, making sure you've covered all four points of the compass (north, south, east, and west) at least once each. When you're done, drop a quarter on the ground at your ending point.

5. Let your friend know she can now look! Then tell her to take up her position at the starting point, next to your evidence marker. Hand her your compass.

6. Now, guide your friend to the quarter while reading aloud the directions you wrote down. See if she can retrace your route, walking in exactly the same directions you did, and with the same number of steps. If she can, she should be standing on the quarter when she's done!

7. Now, switch roles and see if you can follow *her* directions.

Part II. A Few More Points...!

Got the hang of the four points of the compass, rookie? If so, try this to really test your compass skills!

1. Follow the same steps that you did in *Part I*, only *this* time, don't just use north, south, east, and west. Use the following directions as well: northeast, northwest, southeast, and southwest. Mix them up a bit, and remember to vary the number of steps you take! Can your friend find your quarter now? (In fact—can *you* find it now? Or are you out twenty-five cents?)

Detectives use a variety of compasses, like the ones shown here, to help them track suspects.

What's the Real Deal?

"North! He's heading north! Now he turned east! Vehicle turned east onto Lefferts Avenue!"

When police hear a transmission like that, rookie, they usually don't have time to look at a compass—they're too busy giving chase! With this activity, you should have begun to see how the police world gives directions a bit differently than everyone else. Simple statements, like "turning north off of Lefferts Avenue onto Nostrand Avenue," give police an exact picture of what a suspect is doing. Did you feel how, after a bit of practice, the directions began to become natural for you? There's a good chance that now you'll never forget which end of that park is north, and which ends are south, east, and west!

Police and detectives don't carry compasses all the time—and for a very simple reason. Because knowing these compass points is so important, detectives memorize them! Detectives know the area where they work so well that, after a while, saying "he went east" is as natural as saying "in my backyard." Detectives are so used to using these directions, they can direct not only police on the ground toward a fleeing perp, they can direct police vehicles as well. In fact, even a police helicopter can join in the chase while receiving directions from a pursuing officer or detective! That's why these compass points are so powerful, rookie. Whether you're on foot, in a car, or up in the air, they can always be understood. They're the same everywhere!

Tracking Him Down!

Okay, rookie—time to see how well you know your points of the compass!

You and your partner have been conducting a surveillance of a suspect in a string of street robberies to see what you can learn. But in a crowd, you lose not only the perp—but your partner as well!

You get on the radio and contact your partner, who is still **tailing** that suspect. He gives you the following description of where he is, as he follows the suspect from the corner of Hanley Avenue and Lois Lane.

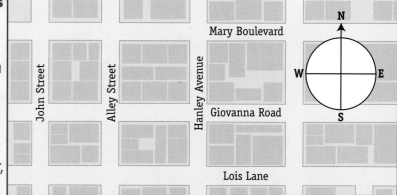

"Okay, I'm still on **the follow**. Suspect is walking north on Hanley Avenue. Suspect has walked two blocks, and now has turned west. Suspect is walking west…he's walked two more blocks, and is now heading south. Suspect has turned south. Suspect has gone one block south. Now suspect is turning east…suspect has gone one block east, and has turned south again. Suspect has gone one block south. Now suspect has stopped. Suspect is stopped at that corner."

So, rookie—relying only on your partner's directions—can you find the suspect? (And when you're done tracing the suspect's route, check *Case Closed* to see if you're on the right corner!).

How to Use Your Compass

There may be no more valuable tracking tool out there, rookie, than a simple, reliable compass! Its batteries won't die (because it doesn't have any!), and as long as you keep it safe and dry—and know how to read it properly—it will never let you down. You'll always know the direction in which you (or your suspect) are moving!

The first thing you need to know about a compass is simply this: The red arrow always points north. If you hold the compass still in the palm of your hand, or put it down on a flat surface, the red point of the needle will always rotate until it's pointing directly north.

Don't be confused if the directional letter "N" (for north) that's printed on the compass doesn't match up to the direction of the red arrow. It doesn't matter where the written letter "N" is—the red arrow *always* points north.

How do you determine which direction you're going? Simple. First, make sure the compass is still and level (if you're holding it, put it in the palm of your hand and try not to shake it). Once the compass needle is steady and pointing north, line up the compass's letter "N" with the needle's red tip. The compass is now "oriented."

Line up the letter "N" with the red tip of the arrow.

Once you've got the compass oriented, just look at the letters around the outside of the compass. While still holding the compass the same way, which letters are you walking toward?

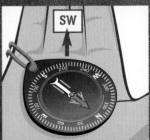

The same principles apply if you're trying to figure out which direction a suspect is walking in. Just orient the compass, then compare the direction your compass points in to the direction the suspect's tracks are going. (And in case you didn't know, N = north, S = south, E = east, and W = west. So if SE = southeast, and NW = northwest, can you figure out what SW and NE mean? You probably can!)

Once the compass is oriented, look at the direction you are facing and determine the direction on the compass. Here, you would be facing southwest (SW).

Out of Sight!

Stuff You'll Need
- A rookie friend
- Compass (DA)
- Notebook (DA)
- Pencil (DA)

Sometimes, rookie, catching up to a **suspect** you've been **tracking** doesn't automatically mean an arrest. If, for instance, you don't have all the evidence you need to make the **collar**—or if you think the suspect might lead you to even *more* suspects—it might be better just to stay hidden and observe the suspect you've been tracking. The art of **surveillance**—of staying out of sight while watching a suspect's every move—is a tactic used *after* a suspect has been tracked down. Surveillance has led to many big arrests and is one of the best tools in a detective's arsenal. So you need to learn how to use it!

Surveillance is often used by detectives who are investigating well-known criminals. For instance, a detective might get a tip that a career burglar has recently been released from jail, and is up to his old tricks. But so far, the burglar hasn't been caught in the act and hasn't left enough evidence to tie him to any of his crimes (this is his *career*, after all—he's probably quite good at it!). In this case, a team of detectives might conduct surveillance on that suspect—secretly following him around, to see what he does all day (and night!). Then, when he steps out of that window with his pockets stuffed with jewelry—*bang!* He's nailed in the act!

Detectives on surveillance might also want to see who this burglar's friends are. So while observing him, they'll take notes of everyone he talks to. This way, they might develop information about other suspects. The main suspect might even lead them to a wanted criminal!

This kind of surveillance works on all sorts of criminals, rookie—not just burglars. That's why it can be such an effective detective tactic. But that doesn't mean it's easy. The art of "seeing without being seen" can be one of the trickiest parts of a detective's job—and it's something that very few people do well.

Are you ready to begin developing your surveillance skills?

What You Do

1. Inform your rookie friend that, sometime over the next week, you're going to be conducting a surveillance on him. Don't tell him when or where, but let him know that for about a half hour, he's going to be under secret observation!

2. Be patient and wait a few days so that your friend lets down his guard. Use that time to plan your surveillance (just as real detectives always do). When is he most likely not to notice you? During recess in the schoolyard? On Saturday at the soccer game? You also have to consider how to stay hidden. Can you wear something that will throw him off, even if he sees you? He's probably familiar with your clothes. Can you borrow a jacket or hat from someone he doesn't know?

3. When you've come up with what you think is the best time and place, conduct your surveillance. Don't get too close to him, and don't try to learn everything about what he does. (You'll be learning some more advanced surveillance techniques in upcoming Case Files!) Just keep a good distance, and watch him without him seeing you.

4. Use your compass to keep precise track of his movements, and make notes in your detective notebook. Your entries could include things like, "Suspect walked south in the soccer field, then walked over to food stand. Subject bought a bottle of water and a hotdog. Suspect wearing blue jeans and a brown sweater."

5. When you're done, wait another day or so, then let your "suspect" friend know that you've already conducted the surveillance.

10/19 4 p.m.

Suspect walked south in the soccer field, then walked over to food stand. Subject bought a bottle of water and a hotdog. Suspect wearing blue

Ask him if he saw you. He'll probably claim he did! But can he prove it? Ask him when you did it. Can he give you the details? Show him your notes to prove he didn't catch you!

More From Detective Squad

If you've got a few rookie friends all practicing surveillance techniques, why not conduct surveillance on each other? Get together a group of three or four fellow trainees, and agree that you're each going to conduct surveillance on one other member of the group at some time over the next week. But don't announce who is going to watch who! When you conduct your own surveillance, remember to keep detailed notes. When the week is over, get together again and compare notes. Did someone conduct a surveillance on you? Were you able to spot them? Did you accidentally bump into a fellow rookie conducting surveillance of the same "suspect" that you were watching? (That's something that happens to real detectives every now and then!)

What's the Real Deal?

With surveillance, rookie, the whole point is to turn yourself into a ghost—someone who can watch a suspect without being watched himself (in fact, "ghost" is a common police nickname for someone conducting surveillance!). With this activity, you got your feet wet with the basics of surveillance. Stay out of sight, don't get too close, don't wear clothes that give you away...and keep those eyes open. Keeping a detailed record of what you see will help you recall it all later, and help you build your case.

Detectives simply could not get along without using surveillance, rookie—it's one of the most common law enforcement tools out there. It's also an especially effective way of going after criminals who are professional and organized. In fact, unless someone gets very lucky and stumbles on a crime-in-progress, the best way for detectives to **take down** an organized criminal gang is to conduct a long-term surveillance on them. That way, detectives can learn as much as possible about the gang, and then arrest not just one of them, but the whole crooked bunch!

DET. HIGH-TECH! Surveillance Gear

Detectives use a great variety of sophisticated equipment to conduct surveillances. Some criminals can be very tough to watch, so police use special equipment to keep an eye on them, while managing to stay out of sight themselves.

Zoom Camera: With the addition of a long "zoom" lens, police can take detailed pictures of a surveillance location from blocks away.

Binoculars: Powerful binoculars can enlarge what police can see by as much as ten times.

Telescope: If police have an **observation post** that allows them to set up something as large as a telescope, they can enlarge what they would normally see by over 100 times.

Eavesdropping Equipment: Special "bugs"—secret microphones—can be hidden in areas as small as the button on a sofa cushion. Some can broadcast the sound they pick up a short distance, to police hidden nearby. Others are "hard-wired"—meaning they have a wire attached to them, which is run inside a wall and to a police tape recorder in another room.

Pinhole Camera: Technology has advanced so far today, rookie, that a camera can be as small as a thin magic marker. A wire run from this tiny hidden camera feeds what the camera sees to police hidden nearby.

GPS Tracker: By using a GPS—Global Positioning System—police can keep track of a particular vehicle. A "transponder" planted on the vehicle broadcasts a signal which tells police where the vehicle is at all times. Some GPS Trackers are even small enough to be hidden in a person's clothes, allowing detectives to keep track of a particular person.

Hiding in Plain Sight

Stuff You'll Need
- **Some changes of clothing**
- **A rookie friend**

A detective technique that's very helpful on a **surveillance** is **disguises**. Remember: The key during a surveillance is not to be noticed. So when a detective is following a **suspect** in a certain area, he'll make sure that he doesn't stand out. And if the suspect is someone who the detective has encountered before—maybe even arrested—a disguise is all the more necessary!

A disguise doesn't have to mean a lot of make-up and clothing changes, rookie. You'd be surprised how just a few little alterations to your appearance can make you blend in. Try this activity to practice "fading into the background"!

What You Do

Part I. Give 'Em the Hook

1. Just like with any other aspect of a surveillance, rookie, you should start with planning. So imagine that you're going to be conducting a surveillance on a subject in a particular place—say, a shopping mall or at a school basketball game... someplace where you think you can blend in with a lot of other people.

2. Next, decide what kind of clothing fits best in that environment. If you're going to your school's basketball game, maybe you should wear a big, loose basketball jersey (maybe even for the other team!). If you're going to be at the local park, try a pair of sweats. If you're going to an upscale shopping mall, dress nicely. The key is not to stand out!

3. Have you ever noticed how different someone can look just by changing their haircut or hairstyle? You can use that to your advantage! If you want to give yourself a slick, groomed look, run some gel through your hair and slick it back off your face. If you're going to a basketball game or to hang out at a local park, you might experiment with combing your hair forward, over your forehead. This will conceal part of your face! If you're a girl, try pinning your hair back, or putting it in a high ponytail. You can even use some temporary "spray-style" hair gel to change the color of your hair. Remember: You don't want to be recognized and **get burned**!

4. Now, it's time for some acting! Along with changing your hair and clothing, you can alter your look a great deal by changing your movements. So practice changing your walk a bit. If you're going to be in an area where you need to be well dressed, walk straight and upright. If you're going to be at a park, put on a baseball cap and practice walking with your head down. Slump your shoulders a bit, as if you're tired from just playing a game. Maybe carry a tennis racket or basketball with you. There are all sorts of options you can use that fit the location—and, at the same time, that change your appearance. But the key movement to change is your walk. Remember: It's the walk that talks!

5. Another great disguise trick is to use a **hook**. This is when you wear something obvious—like a baseball cap, a pair of sunglasses, or a bright shirt—and then suddenly change it. Anybody seeing you for the first time will notice the hook. But later, when you remove the hook, and they see you without it or with a different one—they'll likely think it's a different person!

Part II. Getting Up Close and Personal

Now that you've learned a bit about how to alter your appearance, are you ready to see if you won't be recognized?

1. Pick an upcoming event that you know a friend will be attending. It can be a school event, a sports event, or even something as simple as a shopping trip or an outing to the library to work on a report.

2. Once you've come up with a target suspect and event, plan your disguise. Remember: You want to fit in, but you *don't* want to look like you! So go over some of the suggestions in *Part I* (and some of the disguises you tried), and use them here.

3. When the time comes, **tail** your friend while in disguise. See how close you can get without him noticing you.

4. Make sure you take notes about what your friend is doing. If he's at the library, you can write things like, "Subject got up from table, got a large red book from the stacks on the second floor, and returned to reading table."

5. When you think you've conducted enough surveillance, *really* test your disguise. If you've remained undetected until now, try walking right past your rookie friend. (But don't look him in the eye! A key way to avoid being recognized is avoiding all eye contact!) Now sit or stand right beside your friend. See how long it takes until he recognizes you! (If he *still* doesn't, you can always leave and prove to him later that he was under surveillance by showing him your notes! How shocked will he be then?)

More From Detective Squad

💻 Need a place to log your surveillance notes? Then log on to **www.scholastic.com/detective** to print out your very own surveillance log. There's also a training exercise to complete that will test your ability to spot a disguise!

What's the Real Deal?

By altering your hairstyle, clothes, and walk, you can often fool even people who know you very well. Unless somebody is specifically looking to find you, it's often easier than you might think to pass as a different person. Because people usually don't look hard at other people (especially people they don't immediately recognize), it can be a simple task to blend into the background while conducting a surveillance.

Detectives use disguises of all different types when on a surveillance, rookie, and they use the same tactics that you did. They plan their disguise, taking into consideration where they'll be. So, if they're going to **tail** a suspect on a busy city street, they may dress like construction workers or delivery folk. If they're conducting surveillance in a business area, they may dress professionally and carry briefcases. If they really want to alter their appearance, they might even temporarily color their hair, or men might wear a fake beard (or even grow a real one!).

CASE IN POINT   Disguise Surprise!

In 1999, rookie, police apprehended a woman wanted for nearly three years on a very serious crime—a homicide!

The woman—whose case was featured on the television show "America's Most Wanted"—was an expert in disguise, and changed her appearance constantly while avoiding capture. She also moved around a lot, making it difficult for police to track her down.

But detectives got a break. After her case appeared on TV a second time, police got a tip the woman might be living in the Boston area. They put a suspicious house under surveillance—and learned from a pizza worker making a delivery that the woman was inside!

The bad news was—she wasn't alone. Fearing a confrontation, police needed a way to get inside the house quickly and quietly. They decided to turn the woman's own tricks on her. So a short while later, another pizza delivery was made to the house. The man who answered the door was confused—hadn't the pizza already arrived?

Then the deliveryman charged past him, and into the house—along with a whole squad of armed police officers. This deliveryman was a police officer in disguise!

Detectives discovered the woman inside the house—as usual, in disguise. But they weren't buying it—and she was placed under arrest.

Stuff You'll Need
• A few fellow rookies

Give Yourself a Hand

Very often, rookie, conducting **surveillance** is more than a one-man (or woman) job. In order to avoid being caught when watching a **suspect**, detectives will very often work in teams, switching off from time to time so that one detective isn't observed watching the suspect for too long. That way, even if the suspect gets suspicious, he won't see the same person twice—and so, will probably chalk it up to his imagination!

Here's how it works. Let's say detectives are following a known bank robber as he walks around a small town. The suspect is walking down Main Street—maybe he's looking for the best bank to rob!

Behind him, however, is a detective dressed like a business professional. He's about a half-block behind the suspect, carrying a briefcase and watching his every move. When the suspect goes into a store, the detective waits for him to come out, so he can keep up the surveillance. But what if the suspect happens to spot the detective as he leaves the store?

To throw him off, the detectives will make a switch! The detective will use a special hand movement to signal to one of his fellow detectives to take over the surveillance. He'll drift off into a store or down a side street, while the replacement detective moves closer to the suspect. Now the suspect has a new **tail**—one he hasn't seen before! Here's where having a tail be a "she" instead of a "he" becomes all the more valued. The suspect isn't expecting to see a woman in place of a man!

Lots of detectives will sometimes be used on a surveillance like this, rookie, especially if it's in an area where they might be spotted. While the main detective watches the suspect, he'll also use special hand signals to keep the rest of his team updated as to what the suspect is doing (because many times his teammates are a half-block behind him, and can't even see the suspect!). This way, each detective knows what's going on at all times—and everyone is ready for an emergency, or for one of them to take over the surveillance. The key to this type of surveillance is to switch it up often—and to have good hand signals set up *before* you start (the middle of a surveillance is no time to start discussing signals!).

Try this, so that you'll know your signals—"hands" down!

What You Do

1. As you've learned, rookie, the first step in a surveillance is to decide with your partner on what each hand signal will mean. Detectives usually set up a set of signals among themselves, then stick to the same system. That way, they automatically know what each signal means. So first, practice the following hand signals. As you do them, see if your partner can name what they mean. Then switch up, and see if you can do the same.

- Scratching your lower back: *Suspect is moving.*

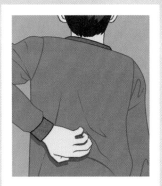

- Your hand down at your side in a fist: *Suspect is moving again.*

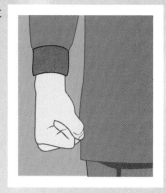

- Pulling on your left ear: *Suspect has made a left turn.*

- Rubbing the back of your head: *I've lost sight of the suspect.*

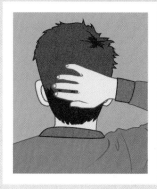

- Pulling on your right ear: *Suspect has made a right turn.*

- Running a hand through your hair: *Time to switch off.*

- Your hand down at your side, with your open palm facing backward: *Suspect has stopped moving.*

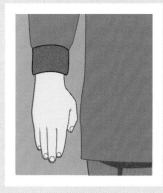

2. Can you think of any other special signals that might be useful when tailing a perp? (How about one for "suspect has entered a store"? Or "suspect is getting into a car"?) But remember: Whatever signal you come up with, it needs to be visible to teammates who are *behind* you—and who are very often a good distance away! (When you're done, check out *Case Closed* for some extra signal possibilities.)

3. Once you've come up with all the signals you think you'll need, quiz each other again to be sure you know them all.

4. Now it's time to put them to work! Tell a friend that you'll be following him a few days before you do, but don't tell him exactly when. Practice your signals by conducting a tail of your friend. Remember to stay far enough back not to be spotted (forty feet, minimum—about the length of three or four cars). Be sure to signal to your partner everything the "suspect" does. Then when you feel you've got the hang of it—but before you think you've been spotted—make the switch and let your partner give it a try. You're now an experienced surveillance team!

In a surveillance, two rookies follow behind their suspect—in this picture, all three are outlined in white so *you* can see who they are!

More From Detective Squad

For some help getting your hand signals down cold, head to **www.scholastic.com/detective**.

What's the Real Deal?

This activity focused on those all-important hand signals, rookie, because it's important for the tailing detective to constantly let her teammates know what's going on. Conducting a surveillance of this type can be tougher than it sounds, so detectives need to be in touch as much as possible. But in cases that don't permit the use of a police radio—cases where the detectives run a serious risk of being spotted, especially if they're seen whispering into a radio—hand signals are the best way to go. You should now have a feel for communicating "by hand"!

In some cases, a real surveillance team might use hidden police radios to keep each other informed. Detectives have access to all sorts of high-tech gadgets—including radios that can be well hidden. With a hidden radio, the tailing detective can keep her teammates informed by quietly talking into a small microphone pinned inside her shirt. But there's a hitch! Not only might this detective be spotted "talking to herself," the radio could also fail to work! All electronic equipment can be tricky, rookie, and sometimes it has a mind of its own. With hand signals, nothing is left to chance. The whole team is working together and is in constant communication. The suspect is not only under surveillance, he's badly outnumbered. So if he tries to commit a crime—like a robbery or burglary, or if he's associating with other criminals and attempts to throw anyone following him off his trail—he doesn't stand a chance!

Teaming Up

Hey, rookie, are you ready to do some real **surveillance**? In *Case File #8: Give Yourself a Hand*, you learned all about the hand signals to use when communicating with your team in the field. But knowing the signals while sitting in your house and knowing them while actually **tailing** someone are two very different things!

Let's see how well you can combine your hand-signal and **disguise** skills in a real-life surveillance. Try the following activity, to see if you and some fellow rookies—a surveillance *team*—can "see without being seen"!

What You Do

1. First, pick a target "**suspect**" that you're going to tail. It should be a friend or family member that you and your team are going to follow over the next couple of days. But don't tell the target about it!

2. Use the next few days to meet with your team and plan your surveillance. Planning is always a basic part of conducting surveillance, rookie—don't neglect it! Remember: The target is a person who knows you. So you'll not only need to use good team surveillance tactics, but you'll have to use your disguise skills as well. (That way, even if you're spotted—you won't be spotted!)

3. Try to do **the follow** on a street or in a shopping mall where a lot of people are walking—a busy area with a lot of foot traffic is best. Once you've acquired your target, the tail is on! Remember to stay far enough back not to be spotted (forty feet, minimum—about the length of three or four cars). Be sure to signal to your partner what the "suspect" does—

including scratching your lower back when the suspect first starts moving.

4. A good way to keep an eye on your suspect while he's stopped is to follow his reflection in a glass window. Find the front window of a store in which you can see your suspect reflected. Pretend to be studying something you want to buy in the store's window display. In reality, what you're doing is watching your suspect without appearing to!

5. After a few minutes, once you feel you've gotten the hang of using your hand signals, signal your partner to make the switch. Conduct the **hand-off** by falling back gradually so that your partner overtakes you. He should walk right by you, but *not* look directly at you. (Remember: You're supposed to be strangers, not members of a surveillance team! So at no point should you appear to be working together—or even to know each other!)

6. Keep handing off to new teammates, until everyone's given it a try. If there are just two of you conducting the surveillance, keep switching off every five minutes or so. Can you keep the surveillance up for a half hour without getting spotted? Were you able to follow the suspect the whole time?

More From Detective Squad

You can practice doing follows like this anytime, rookie—even if a friend or family member isn't available. A local shopping mall (visited with a senior detective) is a great place to practice your surveillance techniques. Just pick a target "suspect" with your partner, and tail that person for awhile. But don't get too close, and don't tail them for too long—twenty minutes is plenty. Then pick a new subject. It's a great way to practice your hand signals and become a surveillance expert! If you do it with friends, be sure to warn them in advance!

What's the Real Deal?

Were you able to follow that relative or friend without being spotted, rookie? Conducting surveillance like this takes a good deal of practice. With this activity, you got the opportunity to use a number of things you've learned. Did your disguises work? Were you able to use the hand signals to keep each other informed of the suspect's movements? Were you able to execute smooth hand-offs? You had a lot of techniques to try, so even if it didn't go smoothly, don't worry. With practice, it will!

Detectives use the same tactics you did in this activity to keep an eye on suspects. They will use a whole team to keep the suspect off balance, and watch him in windows and from a distance. They'll wear disguises and use hand signals. They'll make sure they switch off a lot. To an experienced team on a surveillance, these techniques become second nature. And the proof is in the country's jails. There are thousands upon thousands of **perps** behind bars today who thought they were just "too smart" to ever get caught. Little did they realize that while they were bragging...they were being watched!

A s you probably know, rookie, on September 11, 2001, a group of radical Islamic terrorists hijacked two airplanes and crashed them into the twin towers of the World Trade Center in New York City. The terrorists were part of an organization known as Al Qaeda, led by Osama Bin Laden, a multi-millionaire who is a sworn enemy of the United States. Al Qaeda operatives also crashed a third plane into the Pentagon in Washington, D.C. Shortly thereafter, over Pennsylvania, heroic passengers fought with Al Qaeda operatives to regain control of a *fourth* plane that the operatives had hijacked—resulting in that plane crashing to the ground. In total, more than 3,000 people lost their lives that day as the result of the terrorist attacks.

As a result, detectives in America today are far more alert to anything that might signal planning for a future terrorist operation. For instance, if a **suspect** has identification in a number of different names, or if he has just recently entered the country, a detective might want to question that suspect more closely about his activities. The detective might even look into getting permission from a judge to search that suspect's home, or to examine his phone and financial records. Since September 11, both federal and local law enforcement all over America have also stepped-up their use of **surveillance**, both at home and overseas. Surveillance today is being conducted in ways and places Americans have never seen before. Some of these are:

Airports

If you ever flew on an airplane before September 11, rookie, you probably got to the airport not long before the plane took off. You also probably sailed right through the baggage-loading area. Not anymore. Today, all hand-carried baggage is X-rayed by airport personnel before it's carried onto the plane by a passenger. All bags loaded into the plane's storage area are also X-rayed by sensitive new equipment designed to pick up dangerous objects (like explosives).

There are other types of surveillance going on at airports that may be less obvious to you, rookie. Undercover federal officers often mingle with airport crowds, on the lookout for any sign of trouble or suspicious passengers. There are also plainclothes officers, known as Air Marshals, who look just like "normal" passengers—but who may board a plane carrying guns, in case of any trouble.

Even when you "check in" at the airport to reserve your seat, your name is entered into a computer database to ensure you aren't a wanted person—and to make sure you're not on a "watch list" of people law enforcement consider a potential terrorist threat.

Flight Schools

Before September 11, rookie, it was relatively cheap and easy to learn how to fly a small plane in the United States. Flight schools were free to teach who they wanted, when they wanted. Now, law enforcement keeps a close eye on even small flight schools. Because small planes can be used to spread harmful chemical gasses (a plan Al Qaeda is known to be very interested in), flight schools are now subject to more federal surveillance—and many have been advised by law enforcement to be on the lookout for potential terrorists attempting to learn to fly.

Certain Stores

Some items that were easy to buy before September 11 are now much more difficult to get. For instance, certain types of fertilizer—chemicals used to help crops grow—can also be used to construct very powerful bombs. For that reason, stores that sell large quantities of these types of fertilizer are now advised to report any suspicious customers to law enforcement authorities immediately.

Landmarks, Bridges, and Tunnels

Some places are of tremendous symbolic importance for Americans—like the Statue of Liberty in New York, for instance, or the Lincoln Memorial in Washington, D.C.

Surveillance of these areas has also been stepped up, with plainclothes federal agents and local detectives watching for any sign of suspicious activity near these crowded locations.

The Department of Motor Vehicles

A key for undercover terrorists operating in the United States is to establish a false identity—which often means a fake driver's license. In most states across the country, the Department of Motor Vehicles (which is in charge of issuing drivers' licenses) has changed its licenses to make them tougher to fake. They also have computer systems in place to catch those who have applied for more than one license, using different names.

The Border

While many people still feel America's borders need *more* surveillance, those entering the United States are checked out more completely than in the past. The names of those arriving are entered into computers to see if they are wanted. People from certain nations—mostly in the Middle East—can sometimes be subject to extra surveillance, especially if they are carrying a large amount of luggage.

Not everyone feels this extra surveillance is a good thing, rookie. Some Americans feel the new checks go too far and intrude on the rights of American citizens and visitors. Others feel the checks don't go far enough, and should be increased to prevent further terrorism.

Either way, one thing is certain: After September 11, surveillance in America will never be the same again.

Watch It!

Sometimes, rookie, detectives might not conduct **surveillance** on a *person*, but on a *place* instead. If, for instance, detectives suspect a particular store is buying stolen goods, or a **suspect** is planning a crime and is having other criminals visit him where he lives, detectives will set up a spot where they can watch this location. By setting up an **observation post**, detectives can stay out of sight while watching who goes in and out of the place they suspect of conducting illegal activity. It's a great way to build a case, and gather information about more than one suspect at a time!

The key to an observation post, rookie, is the same as with any surveillance: planning. You need to make sure you're well out of sight, yet can keep a steady eye on the location in question. As usual, you need to figure out how to see without being seen!

What You Do

1. With a fellow rookie, plan your observation post by picking both a location to watch and a particular person to watch there. It can be something like your sister's dance class, your brother's karate school, or another friend's trip to the bicycle store. But come up with a *human* target and a *location* target.

2. Next, together with your rookie friend, **scout** the location you've chosen. Walk by it several times, but try not to show too much obvious interest in it. Remember: Surveillance is supposed to be kept secret! Now, check out the area around the location. Do you see any good spots where you can remain hidden while watching your target? How about across the street, behind a parked van? Can you go into a nearby store and watch through

the window? Behind some trees in a nearby park? You're going to need to find *two* observation posts between the two of you—so look hard!

3. Now, when you know your target person is going to visit the location, you and your fellow rookie take up position beforehand in separate observation posts. Each of you

should observe everyone going into or out of the location, and take notes on everything you see, including what the people in the area are wearing and what they are doing. Stay until you spot your target. Check your watch and note down the exact time your "suspect" first enters your target location!

4. Once your target's been spotted, meet up again with your fellow rookie and compare notes. Who was the better observer? Do your notes match? Did you both observe the target? Do your times match?

More From Detective Squad

Your surveillance skills will be put to the test on-line at **www.scholastic.com/detective**. Log on!

What's the Real Deal?

To really watch a spot well, rookie, you need to be patient. You need to find that hidden observation post that allows you to see your location, and then you need to wait. Until your suspect shows up, there's little more for you to do than sit and look! This activity was all about showing you how the key to running a good observation post is to plan it out and scout the area, and then just be patient and let the "criminal" come to you, rather than you following him.

Detectives go to great lengths to set up effective observation posts. In order to keep an eye on a particular location, detectives will take up positions on roofs, or in the back of delivery trucks, or in vans equipped with darkened windows. They'll sometimes position themselves a great distance away and use binoculars or even a telescope to watch a particular location through a window. Using special electronic gear, they can sometimes even place a tiny hidden camera inside a location, and watch everything that goes on from a nearby room! As with any surveillance, the more hidden the detectives are, the safer the crooks feel. And the safer crooks feel, the more they talk— and the more detectives learn about them! So if a location is used for buying stolen goods, detectives can learn not only about the people *buying* the items, they also can learn about the people *selling* them. And so, detectives may get the chance to apprehend a wanted burglar. Similarly, if detectives are watching a location known for selling drugs, they can get info on who's selling it as well as who's buying it. An observation post is simply a great way to get a picture of the whole criminal landscape.

On the Job: At Work with H. Keith Melton
Surveillance Expert

Rookie, even if **surveillance** seems as simple as just "following someone," in actual practice, the art of secretly observing a **suspect** is no simple task. It often takes a trained, experienced expert to pull it off. An expert like H. Keith Melton!

Here's what Keith had to say about surveillance work in a recent conversation.

What kind of surveillance do you do?

My specialty is teaching how technology is used to aid in the tracking of a target or "rabbit."

Who is the surveillance conducted against?

Surveillance is conducted against all types of suspected criminals. Rather than being exciting, as shown in the movies, real surveillance is often tedious and boring. In fact, the object of surveillance usually is to conduct it without letting the "rabbit" know that he is being watched. In this manner, the suspect (rabbit) may lead you to other suspects, or perhaps to where he has hidden the "loot" from a robbery. Real-world surveillance is best conducted by trained teams of individuals with clandestine communications systems from either fixed or mobile "observation posts." A fixed OP might be in an apartment building that overlooks the "rabbit's" place of work. A mobile OP can be literally anything that moves: cars, planes, helicopters, boats, and even bicycles. Rarely is surveillance conducted by a single person since it would probably be ineffective and the "rabbit" would escape.

How valuable is surveillance?

The ability to conduct surveillance is a core skill used by law enforcement and counterintelligence services throughout the United States. Some crimes are difficult to prove without catching the criminal in the act and surveillance is the way in which we watch the suspect until he commits the crime.

What are some surveillance do's and don'ts?

Many people believe that the suspect being surveilled, if he is aware of the surveillance, should "play games" with the surveillance teams and use "ploys and ruses" to escape. Typical examples of these actions include running traffic lights just before they turn red in order to make the car following you run the red light. Other ruses may include jumping on and off a subway car in an effort to confuse and escape surveillance. Such actions are amateurish and only confirm to the surveillance team that you have something to hide. Once a surveillance team spots such aggressive actions to evade surveillance, they often call in all of their resources to insure the "rabbit" won't get away!

What is a typical day conducting a surveillance like?

How you conduct surveillance and the typical day is determined completely by the movements and the anticipated schedule of the "rabbit" you are following.

On the Job: At Work with Charmaine Harris of the Shadow Wolves

As you've learned, rookie, **tracking** is part of every detective's job. But did you know that there is an elite law enforcement unit that is dedicated *totally* to tracking? They're the best in the business!

The Shadow Wolves is the nickname for one of the most unique police units in the world. Made up of Native Americans from various Indian nations (like Navajo, Sioux, Kiowa, and Omaha), the Shadow Wolves are actually members of U.S. Customs and Border Protection—the agency in charge of policing America's borders.

Because of the outstanding tracking abilities which are part of many Native American cultures, the Shadow Wolves have been charged with policing remote stretches of the desert along the U.S.–Mexican border. The Wolves hunt for signs of people transporting illegal drugs or immigrants into the country. They spend their days hunting **tracks**—and if they find some, they chase the **suspects** down!

"We'll follow them for as long as it takes," says Officer Charmaine Harris, a 5-year member of the Wolves. "Usually, they'll stop to take a rest or something. We'll track them, and once we catch up to them, we'll call in for more Customs Officers for support. Then we'll move in to make the arrests."

On the Job: Tom Brown, Super-Tracker!

Tom Brown has been living and breathing tracking for over 45 years. He currently runs a nationally known tracking school, trains law enforcement groups in tracking, and gets called in to work with police agencies when an expert tracker is needed on a tough case. He got his start in an unusual way: "I grew up in the pine barrens of New Jersey," Tom recalls. "My best friend's grandfather was an Apache Indian, and he taught me the skills of tracking and survival. Apaches are the best trackers in the world—and I've been all over."

If properly trained, how much can you really tell from tracks? "Tracks are not lifeless holes in the ground. For instance, if you stand still, then touch your nose, you'll feel your feet shift. Even if you just take a deep swallow, your feet will shift. A real tracker can see these shifts in the tracks." Can you really tell that much from tracks? "To me," Tom says, "a track is like a fingerprint. It's a portrait. Fingerprints can't tell you height, weight, emotional state, whether a male or a female made them—but tracks can."

Doesn't seem possible, rookie? Tom explains: "On any surface, there's dust and grit. The first rule of tracking: keep the track between you and the source of light, and that track will 'flare' in that dust and grit. You'll see it."

Can just *anybody* learn to track? According to Tom: "I could teach it to you in a week."

Case of the Beach-House Burglary

Rookie, you've caught a serious burglary case, and the only evidence you have are some **tracks** at the scene!

The burglary occurred at a house at Sunset Beach. The owner of the beach house, Frank Dwyer, lives there by himself. He states that when he returned to his house last night after work, he found the place ransacked. He's since determined that cash and an expensive watch are missing from his bedroom—and someone also stole his motorcycle out of the garage.

Part I. The Tracks

As the lead detective, you have the Crime Scene Investigation Unit respond to the scene and take photos. Here's a photo taken of the area outside the house's bedroom window, which Mr. Dwyer discovered broken and open when he returned home.

A search of the inside of the house turns up some dusty tracks in the garage. Here's the CSI photo of them.

Some tracks were also found in the sand near the house's front door. Here's the CSI photo.

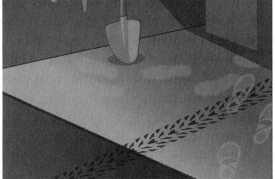

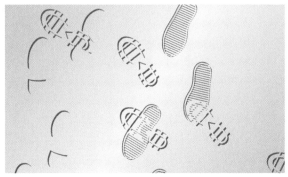

In order to determine which tracks are valuable evidence and which are not, you decide to take **elimination prints** from Mr. Dwyer. He states that he only wears three pairs of shoes on a regular basis, and he provides you with those. Here is a **cast** you made of each of Mr. Dwyer's shoe prints:

Dress Shoes

Sneakers

Work Boots

Part II. The Observation Post

The style of the crime matches a series of burglaries that your detective squad thinks are being committed by a criminal gang known as the "Beach Boys." They're suspected in a recent wave of burglaries in which the thieves target isolated beach houses. You know that the Beach Boys operate out of a broken-down old warehouse on a remote side street, so you set up an **observation post** on a nearby roof to see what you can learn.

At 2:18 in the afternoon, here's what you see outside the warehouse.

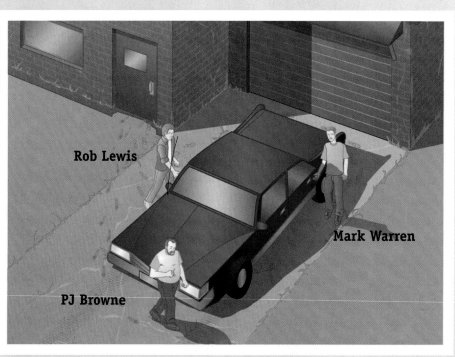

And here, rookie, are pages from the notes you took in the observation post.

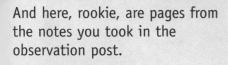

12:35— in position on roof across from warehouse at 86 Old Dune Road. No activity observed. Vehicle with license plates W24-X73 in driveway.
1:00—No activity observed.
1:30—No activity observed.
2:00—No activity observed.
2:18—Three men exited location. One suspect, identified as PJ Browne, entered driver's seat of vehicle. Second suspect, identified as Rob Lewis,

entered front passenger seat. Third suspect, identified as Mark Warren, entered back seat of vehicle. All suspects known members of "Beach Boys" criminal gang. Vehicle then drove off.
2:30—No activity observed. CSI took long-range photos of front of warehouse location

Using special zoom cameras, CSI takes photos of the front of the warehouse location. Here's one, with the **footprints** enlarged.

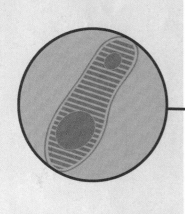

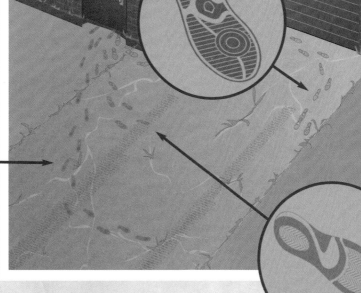

That's all the evidence in the case, rookie. Now—based solely on the track evidence—who among the "Beach Boys" was involved in the beach-house burglary? And if any of these suspects *were* at the original crime scene, can you tell which **perp** took what property? Or were none of them there to begin with?

When you're done, check *Case Closed* for the solution!

CASE CLOSED

Case File #3: Making Tracks pages 19–21

Part I.

Making a cast in grass should have been next to impossible! Now you know where *not* to look for a perp's footprints!

Part II.

Well, rookie, the clearest impression is usually obtained from the print that was made when a person was moving slowest. So your clearest print should be from walking normally. Walking backward should be pretty clear, too—but notice that the tracks are probably deeper in the heel than usual, because you lean on your heels as you walk backward. When you run, the prints are more smudged, and will be deeper in the front of each track, since you push off on the balls of your feet while running (the same goes for hopping in place). And notice when you jump from one spot to another that the track you make as you push off with one foot is a lot like a running track—but the track you make when you land is often messy and unclear, especially if you slid a bit. It all has to do with how fast you were moving and where your weight was when you made the tracks.

Case File #5: Four "Points" You Need to Know! page 26

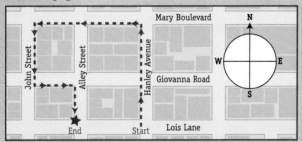

Case File #8: Give Yourself a Hand pages 34–36

Did you come up with any new hand signals? Remember: They should be visible from behind, and easy to remember. So for a suspect getting into a car, how about placing both your hands in each of your back pockets? Or if a suspect enters a store, maybe you could dig in your front pockets, as if looking for money.

Case of the Beach-House Burglary pages 45–47

This was a tough case, rookie, with a lot of steps to solve! Let's start at the beginning:

- Using the samples that Frank Dwyer provided for elimination prints, did you eliminate the correct footprints? Around the window, you should have seen that one set was Frank Dwyer's work boots, but two of the sets didn't match any of Frank's shoes. In the garage, one of the footprint sets matched Frank Dwyer's sneakers, but one set was suspicious. And in the front of the house, all of the prints were made by Frank Dwyer's shoe types. So at the crime scene, you had *two* sets of tracks unidentified by the window, and *one* set in the garage. (And if you were *really* paying attention, you should have noticed that one of the sets outside the window and the set in the garage were the same!)

- Now, the observation post. Well, you know (from your notes) that PJ Browne walked around the front of the car to get into the driver's seat. In the crime scene zoom photo, Browne's tracks don't match *any* of those found at the original crime scene. You also know from your notes that Rob Lewis got in the front passenger seat. The close-up of those tracks matches one of the sets found outside the window *and* to the dusty prints in the garage! And the set of tracks that leads to the car's back seat, you know from your notes, belongs to Mark Warren. And those tracks match to one of the sets outside the window!

- So, your solution: Of the Beach Boys, Rob Lewis and Mark Warren were definitely at the crime scene! And since Rob Lewis's footprints were found in the garage, *he* must have stolen the motorcycle. Which means that while Lewis was doing that, Mark Warren must have been searching the beach house bedroom. So it was Warren who must have found and removed the cash and jewelry. Case closed!